LURE OF STEAM

Up "Merseyside Express" leaves Lime Street, Liverpool.   Re-built
"Royal Scot" 4–6–0 No. 46138 *London Irish Rifleman*.

LURE
of
STEAM

Eric Treacy

First published 1966

This edition published 1995 by
Fraser Stewart Book Wholesale Ltd,
3B Colwell Drive, Abingdon, Oxon
Produced by the Promotional Reprint Company Ltd.

ISBN 1 85648 205 7

Printed in China

Contents

TO

CECIL J. ALLEN

G.O.M. OF RAILWAY JOURNALISTS

in affection and gratitude

Introduction

WHAT more could one ask than to be invited to produce a book about the steam engine; to arrange the pictures oneself; even to use especially favourite pictures that have been published before; in fact, to be given one's head? That was the nature of Ian Allan's invitation to me. Of course, I realise that the invitation came to me as something of a period piece, which is, I suppose, what I am after about thirty-five years activity with a camera hunting the steam engine.

They have been good years, years in which I have made many friends amongst railwaymen; years in which I have had some enchanting days in the country, rejoicing in the peace and beauty of the fells and the open spaces of the north.

Some of my friends think me a bit potty in my addiction to the steam engine, and I suffer a good deal of well-meant condescension as a result of it. But I claim that a man is entitled to be "potty" in his choice of a hobby. After all, it's his business what he does with his spare time. For the life of me, I can't see that it is any more potty to stalk steam engines than deer; or to sit all day in a freezing wind on the muddy bank of a river waiting for fish that aren't there.

In my entry in *Who's Who* I have it mentioned that my hobby is "pottering about locomotive sheds", with the result that when I am introduced to speak at a speech day, a dinner, or a conference, the chairman invariably manages to give the impression that although I have an odd hobby for a bishop, I am (he hopes) in other respects normal.

As my score in years increases, I tend to look back rather than forward: my memories become increasingly precious to me, and I find change more difficult to adjust to. No doubt this accounts for the impatience of the young for the old: it also explains why old people tend to be bores.

As the steam engine has suffered its enforced retirement, I have felt increasingly that this is the end of a pleasant and enjoyable phase in my life, and that the time has come for me, too, to retire from the railway scene, and to find pleasure in other things such as writing, sketching and gardening.

Therefore, the opportunity of doing this book, and the pleasure of preparing and selecting the pictures, have for me a special significance. This is my salute to a magnificent machine—the steam engine: an attempt to show it in all its moods: to recall for my own pleasure, and, I trust, for yours, a phase in the British transport system which has fired the imagination of many, and been the source of great pride to the British people.

The new railways which are taking shape may be economically more viable, operationally more efficient, but I doubt whether they will endear themselves to the public, nor will they inspire the emotional attachment in the same way, or to the same extent, as did the railway in the days of coal and water combining to produce steam.

* * *

The preparation of this book has been great fun, even if it has involved me in a good deal of night shift work. For many weeks, after 10 o'clock in the evening, I have dug into my stock of negatives, and spent a troglodyte existence in my dark room, with sundry interruptions by the telephone, and reminders from my wife that one day was passing into another.

And so, my mind has been carried back to many things no more to be seen or heard . . .

. . . that "curiously rude noise" as Canon Roger Lloyd calls it, peculiar to Great Western engines, which used to come up to the pleasant heights of Kingsland from Shrewsbury Station.

. . . the thunder of an un-rebuilt Royal Scot engine blasting its way up the 1 in 95 from Lime Street to Edge Hill—a noise that literally shook my vicarage in Liverpool.

. . . the sight of a pillar of smoke rising skyward at the north end (or should it be west?) of York Station as an A3 struggled to get its train moving round the station curve.

. . . the murk and sulphurous smell of a large station with steam engines idling their time away between turns of duty.

. . . summer days when one stood lonely on Shap Fell and saw in the distance a plume of steam as the Royal Scot rounded the bend at Tebay, then the long laboured climb with the violence of the exhaust matching the savage weather conditions which often obtained on those wild fells. How right a steam engine seemed on Shap, and, dare I say it, how wrong a grunting diesel-electric seems.

One remembers, too, the extraordinary sense of occasion that accompanied the departure of a steam train from a large station. Although it happened again and again every day, one felt that this was an event.

It started with the first sight one got of the rear end of the locomotive as it sidled down from the shed to the station—especially if it suddenly appeared out of a tunnel as at King's Cross. Then there was the clonk as the engine and its train made contact, the ritual of coupling up, the business that was going on in the cab—the fire to be attended to—gauges to be watched—whisps of steam wreathing round the engine—the simmer of the safety valves: perhaps even a burst of sound as they blew off in spite of the fireman's efforts to keep them quiet. There would be the smell of steam and oil and the sound of the fireman's hammer as he broke up the coal. Then the short conference between the guard and the driver, I imagine, on the subject of weights and measures. There was something Olympian about the driver as he looked out of his cab, a man set apart to control the primitive powers of water and fire, with that power to project 400–500 tons at speeds up to 90 m.p.h. Was there a single passenger who, for a moment, doubted his ability to do this with complete safety?

And, what's more, I suspect that some of these drivers felt themselves to be a superior race. Why not? They had come up the hard way: their authority on their engine was unquestioned: their responsibilities daunting, and their job one that demanded powers of quick decision and a strong nerve. In their years on the footplate, they had battled with the savagery of the elements—fog, snow, wind: and they had had that which is probably the most capricious of all machines to deal with—the steam locomotive. A moody, but handsome beast—that one day would throw its crew about like a bucking horse at a rodeo; another day would be unaccountably short of steam, yet which, more than any other product of the industrial age, had the power to create a personal relationship between itself and those who operated it.

There he is—guardian of the footplate, that most private of places, upon which only the privileged

may be entertained. Then sounds the whistle from the far end of the train, the green flag is waved, the driver's head disappears, gently the regulator is opened. For a moment nothing seems to happen, then, as the exhaust shoots up into the sky, very slowly, the train begins to move.

Yes, indeed, there is atmosphere about this, and there are few people who are not aware of it.

*   *   *

With the departure of the steam engine from the railway scene in Great Britain there will disappear much of the romance of the railway, and its fascination for an enormous number of people, of surprisingly varied backgrounds. There are the railwaymen themselves, many of whom have grown up in the railway service with the steam engine. Perhaps their attitude is something of a love-hate relationship, for oft-times they will have cursed it when it played them up; but, on its day, they have found it to be a machine they could understand and tame, one that would somehow limp home under a firm hand if anything went wrong "under the bonnet"; they found it something essentially simple. Even its dirt and the fact that it was so often facing the wrong way; even its draughts and evil habit of occasionally blowing back were treated as the uglier moods of a creature that had a will of its own, and which defied human efforts to make it behave.

Yes, it may be, that as the steam engine disappears, nostalgia may have blinding effects, so that its sins are forgotten and forgiven, and its virtues magnified.

Housewives, businessmen, dons and beaks, bishops, priests and deacons, lawyers, doctors, old men, young men, soldiers, sailors and airmen, have all, in these latter days, shared with me their sadness that steam is to be no more.

What is the secret of this affection? Is it that the steam engine is so peculiarly British, and that we subconsciously resent its replacement by a machine designed by a Swede?

Or, may it be, that those of us in middle age feel that one of our landmarks is being removed. As one gets older, as I can testify, this removal of things with which we have become familiar, and with which we have come to associate so many personal experiences, can be most disturbing. There are many for whom the sound and sight of the steam engine provokes a host of memories, of separations and re-unions: of holidays and journeyings often: of comforting noises in the night of clankings and chuffings when death stalked in the air: of a pennant of steam marking the passage of a train in some wild valley in the north.

But, I believe that the chief reason for this national act of mourning in respect of the steam engine, this widely felt sense of bereavement, is that, for a large number of people, the steam engine is a thing of beauty. It is not pretty; its beauty is a combination of majesty, aggressiveness and balance. It is the right shape for the job. It is wholly and gloriously itself. It grunts, it belches, and it often protests; it is noisy and massive. By its moods and vigorous sense of life it appeals to something in most of us. As it pounds up a bank like Beattock, you can almost feel with it its travail and hard labour: when it gets over the top, you share its sigh of relief as it coasts down into the lush pastures of the valley of the Clyde.

When a steam locomotive is exerting itself to make up time, you know, beyond any shadow of doubt, that something is happening "up front".

And when you arrive on time having picked up (shall we say?) ten minutes between Peterborough and King's Cross, as you pass the engine and glance at the driver wiping his hands on a piece of cotton waste, you have the feeling not that *he* has done it, but that *we* have done it.

* * *

As I write this introduction I look out from Church House in Wakefield at the precise moment that a sleek Deltic winds across the viaduct with a train from London, and a filthy Stanier Class 5, belching smoke, ducks under the viaduct with a string of coal trucks on the old Lancashire and Yorkshire route.

If you have to have diesel-electric locomotives, then a Deltic is about the best you can get—but what a contrast. A contrast between sleek efficiency and belching, gorgeous inefficiency. For we steam lovers have got to face it—the steam engine is an expensive and inefficient brute by modern standards. The change had to come.

Britain's new railway system will be faster, cleaner, and generally more efficient: in these standards will be reflected the characteristics of the society in which it is set.

It will be characterless. British Rail, as it is shaping, will be devoid of those lovable idiosyncrasies which marked our railways in their earlier days. Gone will be the meandering branch line, the country stations with their neat gardens and air of pastoral leisure. No longer the characters on the footplate who could be relied upon for a virtuoso performance for the benefit of some interested passenger known to them.

It is the resistance to this growing uniformity of the British railway system which is largely responsible for the formation of so many Preservation Societies. Stretches of line along which diverse groups of Englishmen can indulge their passion of playing with trains—life size ones, too. There, on these small stretches of line steam will operate for a few years longer: engines will be cleaner than they have ever been, stations bright and shining, their waiting rooms filled with a variety of relics: amateur railwaymen attired in uniforms which may have seen better days, but which obviously have been "issue" clothing at some time.

I am privileged to be the President of the Keighley and Worth Valley Preservation Society, and there I find an increasing number of steam addicts of all ages gathering at week ends to work their trains from Haworth to Oxenhope, a distance that can easily be walked, but how much more pleasant to chuff up the track behind an L & Y pug, or an ex-Great Northern tank engine.

For me, the latter years of the steam engine have coincided with the richest years of my life; years in which I have been permitted to serve a calling which has taken me to many places, at home and overseas; endowed me with lasting and valued friendships, and given me as deep a satisfaction in his daily work as any man could ask. Years in which my wife and I have shared increasing happiness, in spite of the fact that she has spent many hours parked in all sorts of odd places, whilst her spouse has disappeared "up the line".

There was one occasion, shortly after the end of the last war, when we were visiting Paris and I was exploring the S.N.C.F. I had walked up the line from the Gare du Nord to the sheds at La Chappelle, in the course of which pilgrimage, I had crossed a temporary bridge, replacing one that had been damaged by Allied bombing. On my return, I found that the engineers had removed the bridge! When I returned to our rendezvous at the Gare du Nord, and explained my loss of time of two hours on a trip of about two miles by saying that they had taken the bridge away after I had crossed it, is it small wonder that I had more than usual difficulty in getting my story accepted?

Wives have to be patient with husbands who have hobbies, and some hobbies demand more wifely patience than others! My wife, except for very occasional lapses, has shown exemplary patience, and her lapses have been understandable. After all, what woman wants to see her carpets spotted with chemical stains, or to find her airing cupboard festooned with drying film, or to be driven at high speed along some country road in order to rendezvous with the Royal Scot at Beattock Summit? But she has taken it all remarkably well, and I propose to reward her appropriately and adequately with the "takings" from this book!

So it is, because the steam locomotive is bound up with these happy years in my life, this book is, for me, a retrospect of good things. Of days in the sun; of days in the beautiful British countryside; of soakings and scorchings at the hands of the not-so-beautiful British climate; of contacts with a rich variety of people; of the satisfaction of a hobby that harms nobody, gives pleasure to many, and permits a certain degree of artistic expression.

*   *   *

This book is a kind of pictorial anthology. There is much in it that has been published before, and for that, I ask indulgence, as this is really a personal selection in which I have included pictures that appeal to me, and which have particularly pleasant associations for me. I am encouraged in this by the many letters that I have received suggesting that I should produce in one volume my best photographs of the railway scene in the great days of steam.

The sections in this book have almost arranged themselves. It is natural that as a Northerner, I should start with the two main exits to the north. I have lived east and west of the Pennines, therefore Euston and King's Cross have become familiar places in my travelling life. I have footplated to and from both stations. I have seen the dawn break over Euston as I journeyed homewards on leave during the war, and how many times have I, since the war, sprinted the last hundred yards to King's Cross to catch the 6.40 p.m. to Leeds.

I can anticipate the criticism that this book refers to the north more than the south. I have done my best to give place to the Southern and Western Regions, but I cannot expect those who have special affection for either of these regions to be satisfied. But what can a Northerner do? My expeditions southwards are few, and are nearly always confined to official business, when I can only snatch a few minutes at the termini or adjacent sheds. I must confess that my natural inclination on holiday is to travel north, which explains the large number of photographs taken north of a line from the Mersey to the Humber. However, this is a personal collec-

tion, and has the defects, and perhaps some of the advantages, of a personal view of the subject.

I would run the risk of saying that the north is more photogenic than the south. The country between Settle and Appleby; the open moorland of Shap Fell and the wooded slopes of Beattock; the beauty of the Lowland country through which the Waverley route runs—all provide a wonderful back-cloth for photography, as, I hope, some of the photographs in this book reveal. The industrial scene is not without its appeal too. This I have tried to capture with my pictures in the Pennines, and around Leeds and Newcastle.

I have included a few pictures of French Pacifics in order to show the difference between the British and Continental design. Surely, there never was a more chaste design than that of the British steam engine. There is a brazen untidiness, for instance, about a French Pacific with so much of its vitals revealed, whereas there is modesty about an A3 in its original state, with everything decently tucked away.

There are those, no doubt, who will be curious to know something about the apparatus used to take these photographs. They have been taken with a variety of cameras, some plate, some film; some large, some miniature. The two cameras that have given me the greatest joy to use, and have been entirely reliable, are my Super Ikonta and my Rolleiflex, each fitted with Zeiss lenses.

As I conclude this introduction, I would mention with gratitude the help given me by the officials of the various regions in which these photographs were taken. Press and publicity officers have arranged permits, motive power superintendents have produced beautifully clean engines for me to travel on, and have often seen me off on my journeyings. Ronald Taylor, D.M.P.S. at Leeds has even accompanied me on one of my footplate journeys. Drivers and firemen have helped me with smoke effects, but, perhaps, the least said about this the better in these days of clean air campaigns. Many of the Leeds and Liverpool drivers (from Neville Hill, Copley Hill, Holbeck and Edge Hill) have been kindly hosts on their footplates. To one and all who have made me an honorary member of the railway community, and have given me so so much pleasure during the years of steam, my greetings and thanks.

ERIC TREACY

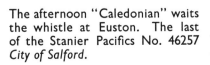

A4 Pacific No. 60007 *Sir Nigel Gresley* waits to set out for the north from King's Cross.

The afternoon "Caledonian" waits the whistle at Euston. The last of the Stanier Pacifics No. 46257 *City of Salford.*

Morning arrivals at Euston. *Left:* Re-built "Patriot" No. 45514 *Holyhead.* *Right:* "Jubilee" 4–6–0 No. 45603 *Solomon Islands.*

Left: A4 No. 60028 *Walter K. Whigham* waits at Belle Isle to back down for duty on the down "Elizabethan".

Below: **Transition at King's Cross.** A1 Pacific and diesel-electric locomotives.

Blue Peter A2 Pacific No. 60532 plunges into Gas Works Tunnel with King's Cross-Glasgow train.

The Rifle Brigade, re-built "Royal Scot" 4–6–0 No. 46146 at Euston with an afternoon train for Manchester.

Flying start at Camden Bank. "Jubilee" 4–6–0 No. 45703 *Thunderer* with the down "Midlander".

Between the Tunnels. A4 No. 60024 *Kingfisher* hustles the down "Elizabethan" up the bank.

A2/3 Pacific No. 60524 *Herringbone* emerges from Gas Works Tunnel with morning train for Glasgow.

Ted Hailstone bursts out of King's Cross with the down Tees-Tyne Pullman behind A4 No. 60014 *Silver Link*.

Above: Approaching Copenhagen Tunnel with the "10 o'clock" A4 No. 60007 *Sir Nigel Gresley.*

Opposite top: Evening at Camden Sheds.

Below: A gleaming "Princess" (No. 46208 *Princess Helena Victoria*) sets out from Euston for Liverpool with the down "Merseyside Express".

Opposite below: Morning at King's Cross Sheds.

Above: Summer evening in North London. A1 Pacific No. 60117 *Bois Roussel* en route for Leeds and Bradford.

Left: Sir Ralph Wedgewood A4 No. 60006 at Holloway with morning train from King's Cross to the West Riding.

Opposite: Blasting up Camden Bank. "Princess" Pacific No. 46208 *Princess Helena Victoria* gets hold of the down "Merseyside Express".

Above: "Jubilee" No. 45733 *Novelty* clambers up Camden Bank with the down "Midlander".

Right: "Princess" Pacific No. 46208 *Princess Helena Victoria* and re-built "Scot" No. 46115 *Scots Guardsman* poke their noses out of Camden Shed.

Opposite: A3 Pacific No. 60055 *Woolwinder* slogs its way up the bank out of King's Cross with the down "White Rose".

The Tetrarch A3 No. 60060 approaches Copenhagen Tunnel with a down excursion train.

Footplate view from *City of Coventry* as it passes Camden Shed with the down "Royal Scot".

Top: No. 69492 N2 0–6–2 with a train of empty stock (not bound for Hatfield!).

Centre: No. 80085 class 4MT 2–6–4 lifts a train for Bletchley out of Euston.

Left: No. 68840 J52/2 0–6–0T shunts freight in the King's Cross Yards.

23

Hard work up the hill at Holloway. A3 No. 60067
Ladas takes the 10.20 a.m. from King's Cross to
Yorkshire.

Pre-war at Queen's Park. No. 46221 *Queen Elizabeth*
with the down "Coronation Scot".

With steam to spare. Re-built "Patriot" No. 45522 *Prestatyn* breasts the hill from Euston with a train for Manchester.

Pre-war at Finsbury Park. A4 *Golden Fleece* No. 4482 with the down "Flying Scotsman".

Princess Margaret Rose has her thirst quenched at Camden Shed.

Sir Nigel Gresley A4 No. 60007 makes a smart start from King's Cross with the down "Yorkshire Pullman".

Swaziland "Jubilee" No. 45630 goes steadily up the Camden Bank with train for Bletchley.

Above: Garnock's Engine. K4 *The Great Marquess* at Leeds City. This engine has recently been purchased by Viscount Garnock.

Left: Class 4MT 2–6–4 No. 42409 designed by Sir Henry Fowler.

Lower left: Class 2P 0–4–4T No. 55237 designed by Pickersgill.

Lower right: Class 2P 2–4–2T No. 50686 designed by Aspinall.

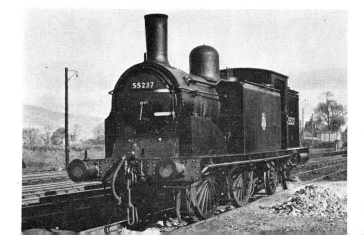

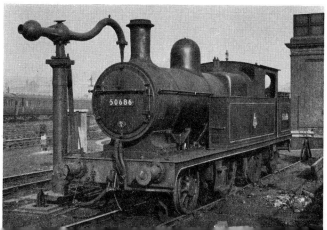

Trio at York. On the right, ex G.C. 4–6–0 class B7 No. 1390.

Class 9F 2–10–0 B.R. freight engine No. 92221.

Class B12 4–6–0 No. 61538. Gresley re-build of Holden G.E. design.

Top: Class D49/2 4–4–0 No. 62736 *The Bramham Moor.*

Centre: County class 4–6–0 No. 1024 *County of Pembroke.*

Below: Johnson 3-cyl. compound 4–4–0 No. 41086.

"Jubilee" class 4–6–0 designed by Stanier. No. 45688 *Polyphemus*.

Two B.R. Standard class 5 4–6–0s; No. 73079 and No. 73053 at Derby.

"Royal Scot" engine as originally designed by Sir Henry Fowler, except for addition of smoke deflectors, No. 6118 *Royal Welch Fusilier*.

Above: "Royal Scot" engine as re-built by Sir William Stanier. No. 6108 *Seaforth Highlander* in black livery.

Below: "Royal Scot" engine in final form, fitted with smoke deflectors, No. 46104 *Scottish Borderer* in green livery.

Above: A4 Pacific No. 60028 *Walter K. Whigham* waits to report at King's Cross for its morning turn to the north.

Right: One of Stanier's Black 5s 4–6–0 No. 45421.

Lower right: Class N15X 4–6–0 No. 2329 *Stephenson*.

Bottom left: Class O1 0–6–0T No. 31178.

Previous page: Pacific Snout I. A4 No. 60009 *Union of South Africa* at King's Cross on down "Capitals".

Top: Pacific Snout II. Front end of L.M.S. "Coronation" Pacific at Crewe.

Centre: Front end of re-built "Scot" No. 46146 *The Rifle Brigade* at Holyhead.

Below: Front end of Stanier Pacific No. 46250 *City of Lichfield* at Carlisle, Upperby.

B1 and A1 waiting to enter Edinburgh Waverley.

Back end view of Class IP 0–4–2, tank engine No. 46701
Bangor, North Wales.

The Nostrils of A2/3 No. 60524 *Herringbone* at King's Cross.

Left: Brewing up. No. 46221 *Queen Elizabeth* at Carlisle, Upperby, service stop for change of crews.

Right: A bit of slipping at Leeds Central. A1 Pacific No. 60130 *Kestrel*.

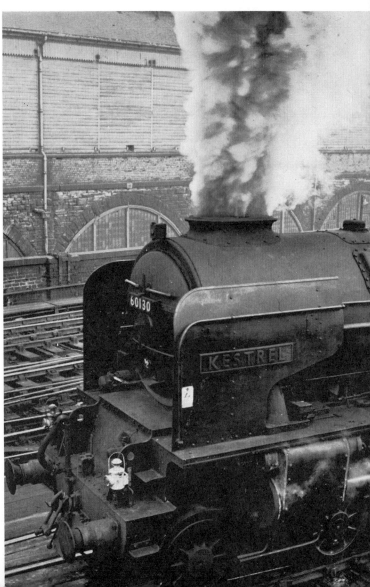

Above: Ex-Caledonian 0–6–0 begins the climb to Beattock Summit from Beattock Station.

Top right: Front end of A1 No. 60156 *Great Central* on the turntable at King's Cross.

Right: I haven't the faintest how and when I got this one! It is obvious what it is.

Top: "Britannia" Pacific No. 70035 *Rudyard Kipling* marks time at a signal near Leeds.

Centre: "Duchess" Pacific No. 46221 *Queen Elizabeth* puffs away from Carlisle with up "Royal Scot".

Right: Business end of "Jubilee" 4–6–0 No. 45681 *Aboukir* at Leeds.

Study in curves at King's Cross. A4 Pacific No. 60009 *Union of South Africa*.

Decorated front of "Merchant Navy" Pacific at Victoria on the down "Golden Arrow".

Aggressive front end. Re-built "Scot" No. 46112 *Sherwood Forester*.

Graceful front end. A3 Pacific No. 60053 *Sansovino*.

Opposite: Some preliminary winding before running Crosti-boilered 2–10–0 on to the turntable at Holbeck M.P.D.

Above: The man with the oil can at Camden Shed. On the left, re-built "Scot" No. 46115 *Scots Guardsman:* on the right, No. 46208 *Princess Helena Victoria.*

Right: Stage set for some maintenance at King's Cross Shed. A4 Pacific No. 60017 *Silver Fox.*

Three views in York Motive Power Depot.

Midday in York M.P.D.

Outside cylinders and motion of 2–10–0 freight
engine in Holbeck M.P.D.

Opposite above: Early morning in Holbeck M.P.D.

Above: Sunlight and Shadow in Holbeck M.P.D.

Opposite below: Locomotive Parade in Holbeck M.P.D.

Below: Neville Hill, Leeds M.P.D.

Above: Getting to work on a BI at Holbeck.

Below left: No. 45573 *Newfoundland* and a 2–10–0 freight engine waiting to go off shed at Holbeck.

Below right: A4 No. 60033 *Seagull* at Grantham M.P.D.

Top: Another view of *Seagull* at Grantham—all ready for the road.

Centre: Doncaster M.P.D.

Left: Driving wheels of No. 4472 *Flying Scotsman* in Doncaster Shed.

Above: A couple of "Scots" and a "Jubilee" at Edge Hill M.P.D. Liverpool.

Left: 0–6–0 No. 47519 (a Jinty tank) at Edge Hill.

Top: No. 46220 *Coronation* emerges from Upperby shed to take an up Perth train from Carlisle Citadel.

With the blower on. Stanier Pacific No. 46250 *City of Lichfield* on the turntable at Carlisle, Upperby M.P.D.

Two views at Carstairs M.P.D.

Top: Grooming at Haymarket. Left, A2 Pacific No. 60535 *Hornets Beauty;* Right, K3/2 No. 61987.

Centre: Morning at Fort William M.P.D.

Right: Morning at Haymarket M.P.D., Edinburgh.

Down "Yorkshire Pullman" approaches Potters Bar Station behind Gresley Pacific No. 4481.

Top: A3 Pacific No. 60112 *St. Simon* nears Potters Bar with train for Peterborough.

Left: Gleaming A4 No. 60007 *Sir Nigel Gresley* streaks along near Abbott's Ripton with up "Flying Scotsman".

Below: An A3 Pacific in its final form (horrible sight!) No. 60035 *Windsor Lad* passes Hadley Wood with express for the north.

Above: An A4 on freight duty No. 60028 *Walter K. Whigham* at Abbott's Ripton.

Right: Group at Peterborough North on the occasion of one of my footplate trips to London. Driver Bill Hoole and Inspector Goodhand in the centre.

Below: After steam ... this. Brush Type 4 diesel electric locomotive approaches Peterborough North with a train for West Riding.

Alone in its class. Class W1 4–6–4 No. 60700 climbs Stoke Bank with up Newcastle train.

Class B12. 4–6–0 No. 61565 south of Grantham with stopping train for Peterborough.

A3 No. 60053 *Sansovino* at Grantham M.P.D.

Grantham Station 1. Train for Nottingham leaves the station behind K2 2–6–0 No. 61771, as express from the south rushes through the station behind A1 Pacific No. 60123 *H. A. Ivatt*.

Grantham Station 2. *Walter K. Whigham* A4 No. 60028 starts a down express for Newcastle from the station.

Right: **Topping up 1.** A few more gallons for the tender of an A4 Pacific at Edinburgh Haymarket M.P.D. before working the up "Elizabethan".

Below: **Topping up 2.** Some extra cobs of coal under the coaling plant at King's Cross M.P.D. for an A4 Pacific about to work the down "Elizabethan".

Below: In the Edinburgh Waverley East Box.

Right: Driver Bill Hoole is "put in the picture" by the guard of the 9.50 a.m. Leeds Central to King's Cross.

Bottom: Shunter Arthur Crabbe connects A4 *Lord Farringdon* to its train at Leeds Central.

Above: Dornoch Firth No. 70054 receives attention at Holbeck M.P.D. on the occasion of my footplate run to Carlisle in 1961.

Right: Driver Tommy Gibbs of Holbeck at work with the oil can on No. 70054.

Below: A Station Inspector at Euston bestows a critical look on the Pacific which has brought in the up "Caledonian". Could it have been cleaner?

The Headboard is placed in position on *Dornoch Firth* before working the down "Thames-Clyde" from Leeds to Glasgow.

Driver Ingelson of Neville Hill has his hand on the regulator as A3
Pacific No. 60036 *Colombo* leaves York with the down North Briton.

Lord Farringdon A4 No. 60034 points his nose northwards with the down "Yorkshire Pullman".

Afternoon Pullman from "the Cross" 1. Down "Tees-Tyne"
approaches Belle Isle Signal Box. A4 Pacific No. 60026 *Miles Beevor*.

Afternoon Pullman from "the Cross" 2. Down "Yorkshire
Pullman" passes Belle Isle Box. A3 Pacific No. 60039 *Sandwich*.

Above: Down "Yorkshire Pullman" leaves King's Cross. A4 No. 60014 *Silver Link.*

Right: Up "Yorkshire Pullman" leaves Leeds Central. A1 No. 60141 *Abbotsford.*

Opposite above: Down "Tees-Tyne Pullman" leaves King's Cross. A4 No. 60022 *Mallard.*

Opposite below: Up "Tees-Tyne Pullman" leaves Newcastle. A4 No. 60028 *W. K. Whigham.*

Down "Queen of Scots Pullman" at Wortley Junction. A3 No. 60086 *Gainsborough*.

Up "Queen of Scots Pullman" leaves Edinburgh. A2 No. 60536 *Trimbush*.

Up "Golden Arrow" at Hilden-borough. "Britannia" No. 70004 *William Shakespeare*.

Down "Golden Arrow" leaving Victoria. "West Country" Pacific No. 34038 *Lynton*.

The original! No. 46100 *The Royal Scot* leaves Chester with the down "Welshman".

Newly turned out in black livery and with smoke deflectors, re-built "Scot" No. 6115 *Scots Guardsman* at Chester with parcels train.

Irish Mail 1. Soon after nationalisation, No. 46127 *Old Contemptibles* threads the City Walls at Chester.

Irish Mail 2. Nicely spot-lighted by the sun, re-built "Scot" No. 46132 *King's Regiment, Liverpool*, leaves Chester with the down "Mail".

Train from Bangor approaching Chester, B.R. Standard class 5
No. 73073.

An unidentified 4–4–0 compound leaves Chester for the North
Wales Coast.

Rebuilt "Scot" No. 46136 *The Border Regiment* backs out of Bangor Shed to take an evening train for the South.

Train for Birkenhead leaves Chester General Station. Stanier Class 5 MT 2–6–0 No. 42961.

Left: Compound 4–4–0 No. 41086 at Llandudno, heads a train for Liverpool.

Above: Class 3F 0–6–0 No. 52230 marshals a freight train in the Bangor Station yard.

Below: Western Region 2–8–0 No. 3828 threads the Chester Tunnels with a freight train for Saltney.

Right: Class IP 2–4–2T No. 46701 at Bangor.

Facing page, top: Up **"Irish Mail"** passes Bangor. Re-built "Scot" No. 46157 *The Royal Artilleryman.*

Facing page, bottom: Holyhead train at Bangor Station. Class 5MT 4–6–0 No. 44766 fitted with Timken roller bearings and double chimney.

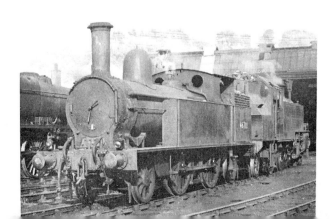

Above: Train for Holyhead leaves Bangor. Class 5 MT4–6–0 No. 44766.

Left: "Horse and Carriage" train climbs the bank from Holyhead Station. Re-built "Scot" No. 46132. *The King's Regiment, Liverpool.*

Head-on view of "Castle"
class 4–6–0 No. 7021
Haverfordwest Castle.

Above: Ranelagh Road Yards I. A "King" 4–6–0 keeps company with a "6100" class 2–6–2T. No. 6115.

Right: Ranelagh Road Yards II. "Castle" No. 5063 *Earl Baldwin* waits its turn on the turntable with a "Britannia" Pacific.

Above: A "King" awaits the right away at Paddington with a train for Wolverhampton.

Below: A "Castle" comes to rest in Paddington with a train from Worcester. No. 7006 *Lydford Castle.*

Above: "Castle" class 4–6–0 No. 5075 *Wellington* at Chester.

Right: *Lydford Castle* No. 7006 receives attention before leaving with an express from Paddington to Worcester.

Below: Scene at Salop. "Britannia" No. 70022 *Tornado* about to come off a train from Swansea to Birkenhead. On the left No. 44687 4–6–0 about to leave with train for Crewe.

Above: Storming start from Paddington. "Castle" class No. 5070 *Sir Daniel Gooch* with a train for Hereford.

Left: "Castle" No. 5092 *Tresco Abbey* leaves Moreton in the Marsh with a train for Paddington.

Exits from Paddington I. "King" class 4–6–0 No. 6011 *King James 1st* with a train for Wolverhampton.

Exits from Paddington II. "Britannia" Pacific No. 70026 *Polar Star* with a train for South Wales.

Above: "Hall" class 4–6–0 No. 6923 *Croxteth Hall* leaves Shrewsbury for Chester and Birkenhead.

Below: On the curve out of Chester General Station, "Hall" class 4–6–0 No. 5916 *Trinity Hall* with a train for Shrewsbury.

Under the coaling plant at Holbeck, Leeds. A3 Pacific No. 60081 *Shotover*.

Above: Two hungry tenders are replenished at King's Cross Shed. *Left*, A4 Pacific No. 60026 *Miles Beevor*; *right*, class L1 2–6–4T No. 67780.

Left: "Merchant Navy" Pacific No. 35028 *Clan Line* tops up at Nine Elms.

Turntable shots II. Stanier class 5MT 4-6-0 No. 44662 on the turntable at Holbeck M.P.D.

Turntable shots III. 2–6–4 Tank engine in the midday sun at Holbeck, Leeds.

Turntable shots IV. *Right:* "Castle" class 4–6–0 No. 5045 *Earl of Dudley* at Paddington.

Turntable shots V. *Below:* "Stanier" Pacific No. 46226 *Duchess of Norfolk* at Kingmoor, Carlisle.

Thirst quenching I. *Above:* A1 Pacific 60118 *Archibald Sturrock* at King's Cross.

Thirst quenching II. *Below:* Rebuilt "Patriot" No. 45535 *Sir Herbert Walker* at Leeds City.

Thirst quenching III. *Above:* B.R. Standard class 5 4–6–0 No. 73171 at York.

Thirst quenching IV. *Right:* ex-W.D. 2–8–0 No. 90070 at the York South freight yards.

Above: "Jubilee" 4–6–0 No. 45639 *Raleigh* rumbles off the turntable at Holbeck.

Left: A4 Pacific No. 60022 *Mallard* de-clinkers at Copley Hill, Leeds.

Above: One of the eight streamlined 4–6–4s of Nord Region. No. 232. S. 002, a four-cylinder Compound at the Gare du Nord, Paris, with the "Nord Express".

Right: Two four-cylinder Compound Pacifics as re-built by Chapelon at the La Chappelle Sheds, Paris.

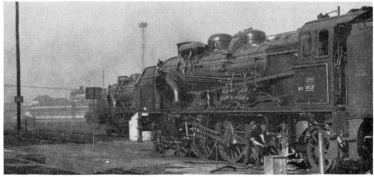

Above: Another view of a Chapelon Pacific at La Chappelle No. 231. E. 31.

Facing page: An impressive front end. Chapelon Pacific No. 231. E. 31 at La Chappelle.

Below: A "Nord" Pacific No. 231. D. 663 at Rouen.

Not much French grace about this ! No. 230. A. 165 with a local
train in the Gare St. Lazaire.

Before and after Improvement (certainly not in looks) I. *Above:* "Gresley" Pacific No. 60056. *Centenary* at Copley Hill.

Before and after II. *Left:* "Gresley" Pacific No. 60074 *Harvester* at Wortley Junction.

Study in Chimneys. A4 Pacific No. 60026 *Miles Beevor* and A1 Pacific No. 60141 *Abbotsford* at Copley Hill.

Pacifics at Nine Elms, Southern Region Re-built Bulleid Pacific No. 35082 *Clan Line* and Re-built West Country Pacific No. 34024 *Tamar Valley*.

Pegler's Pacific. No. 4472 *Flying Scotsman* is prepared for one of its special assignments at Doncaster M.P.D.

A4 Pacific No. 60003
Andrew McCosh takes
coal at Grantham.

A2 Pacific No. 60537
Bachelor's Button at Haymarket M.P.D.

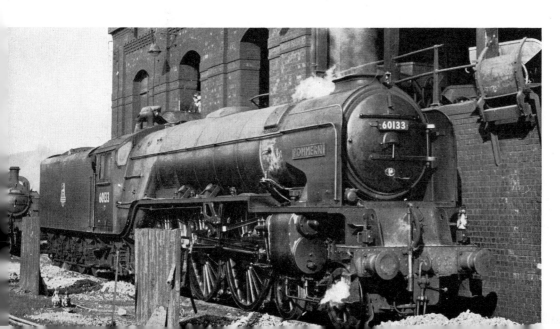

A1 Pacific No. 60133
Pommern at Copley
Hill M.P.D.

97

LMS Pacifics I. *Above,* One of Stanier's streamlined Pacifics No. 6229 *Duchess of Hamilton* in workshop grey at Edge Hill.

LMS Pacifics II. *Below:* Re-built from the Turbomotive, No. 46202 *Princess Anne.* This engine perished in the Harrow disaster.

LMS Pacifics III. *Above:* An evening shot at
Crewe North of Pacific No. 46255 *City of Hereford.*

LMS Pacifics IV. *Below:* Prepared for the down
Royal Scot from Carlisle. Pacific No. 46223 *Princess
Alice.* This engine was originally stream-lined.

Above: One of Bulleid's West Country Pacifics No. 34005 *Barnstaple.*

Below: A re-built Battle of Britain Pacific at Nine Elms, No. 34082 *615 Squadron.*

B.R. Standard Pacific I. *Above:* "Britannia" No. 70051, later named *Firth of Forth*, at Carlisle.

B.R. Standard Pacific II. *Below:* "Clan" No. 72001 *Clan Cameron* at Princes Street, Edinburgh.

Above: Top of the Hill. A typical Caledonian signal box at Beattock Summit.

Facing page: Leeds "B" Box's down starter signal.

Below: Upright pedestal cranks at Portobello East Box.

An impressive example of North British signal box building at
Portobello East, Edinburgh.

Above: The Gateshead Breakdown Crane hauled by
J72 0–6–0T No. 68744.

Below: The York Breakdown Crane.

Record of a Record. Plaque on the boiler of No. 60022 *Mallard*.

"Midships" on a "Britannia" Pacific No. 70022, *Tornado* at Upperby, Carlisle M.P.D.

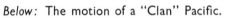

Below: The motion of a "Clan" Pacific.

Above: "Britannia" Pacific No. 70004 *William Shakespeare* at Victoria Station on the down Golden Arrow.

Left: "Schools" class 4–4–0 No. 903 *Charterhouse* on a Hastings to Charing Cross train between Tonbridge and Sevenoaks.

Victoria I. *Above*, the down Golden Arrow leaves Victoria for Dover. "Britannia" Pacific 70004 *William Shakespeare*.

Victoria II. *Below:* Thanet Coast Express leaves Victoria. "Battle of Britain" Pacific No. 34064 *Fighter Command*.

Victoria III. *Above:* "Morning Glory". Down Golden Arrow climbs the bank out of Victoria behind "Bulleid" Pacific 21C157.

Below: Dover Shed. Class Q1 0–6–0 No. 33016 and Class N 2–6–0 No. 31819

Left: Nine Elms Shed. West Country Pacific No. 34001 *Exeter*.

Below: Approaching Hilldenborough. "Schools" Class 4–4–0 No. 30924 *Haileybury* with Hastings to Charing Cross train.

Above: Nine Elms Shed. "Battle of Britain" Pacific No. 34066 *Spitfire*.

Below: Through the Weald of Kent. Class E1 4–4–0 No. 1506 with a parcels train for Charing Cross.

Waterloo I. *Above:* "West Country" Pacific (un-rebuilt) No. 34010 *Sidmouth* with a boat train.

Waterloo II. *Below:* "West Country" Pacific (re-built) No. 34093 *Saunton* with a train for Ilfracombe.

Right: "Stanier" Class 5MT 4–6–0 No. 45219 at Halifax with the up South Yorkshireman.

Below: An east bound coal train leaves Healey Mills Marshalling Yards near Wakefield behind an ex-W.D. 2–8–0.

Above: A "B.R. Standard class 5" leaves Sowerby Bridge with a Liverpool Exchange to Newcastle train.

Below: At Bradley, near Huddersfield. Re-built "Patriot" No. 45535 *Sir Herbert Walker* with a Liverpool to Newcastle, overtakes a freight train behind a "Crab" 2–6–0.

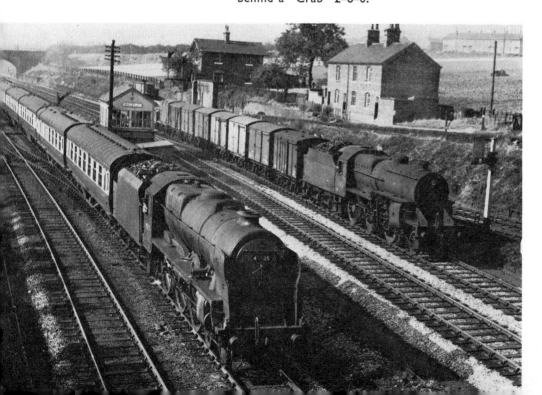

Above: At Luddendenfoot, near Halifax. A "Crab" 2–6–0 No. 42789 pilots a "Jubilee" 4–6–0 with an afternoon parcels train.

Below: At Linthwaite, near Huddersfield. A Newcastle to Liverpool train climbs up to Standedge. 4–4–0 Compound No. 41160 pilots a "Black" 5.

Above: A coal train travels east through Mirfield behind a "Black" 5 4–6–0.

Right: On the Power Station roundabout. Two ex-W.D. 2–8–0s No. 90321 and No. 90165 pass each other near Crofton.

Left: Leaving Huddersfield for Penistone, Class 4P 2–6–4T No. 42384.

Above: Class 7F 0–8–0 Fowler designed freight engine No. 49674 on a coal train at Hebden Bridge.

Below: At Marley Junction, near Keighley. 0–6–0 No. 3078 pilots class 5MT No. 5392 on a Leeds to Morecambe train.

Above: Ex L and Y 2–4–2T No. 50777 on a local train at Mytholmroyd.

Below: Ex L and Y 0–6–0 No. 52411 trundles back to the Shed at Sowerby Bridge.

Leeds and Bradford to Liverpool Exchange train passes Sowerby Bridge M.P.D. behind class 5MT No. 44694.

Museum of British Transport at Clapham. General view from the entrance.

Above: The Fastest of them all. Gresley's Pacific No. 4468 *Mallard* dominates the exhibition.

Right: Two front ends. Gresley's *Mallard* in massive contrast to Metropolitan Railway No. 23, a Beyer Peacock 4–4–0 condensing tank engine.

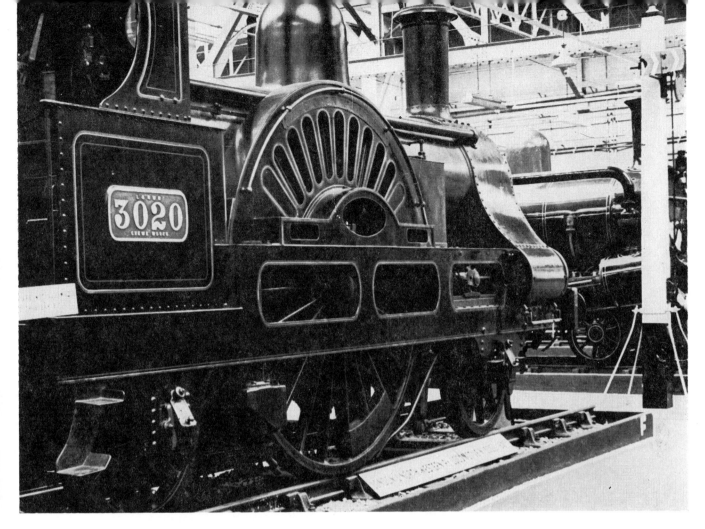

Francis Trevithick's 2–2–0 No. 3020 *Cornwall*.

Wainwright's "D" class 4–4–0 No. 737 as designed for the S.E. & C.R.

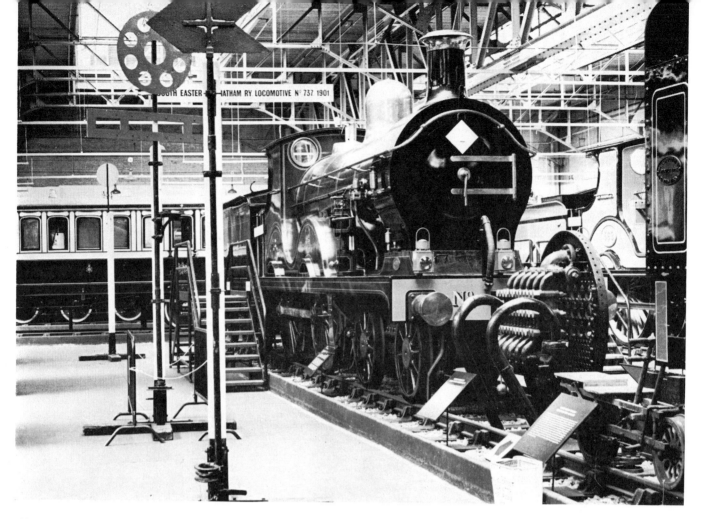

Above: Another view of Wainwright's beautiful 4–4–0 No. 737.

Below: Liverpool and Manchester Railway Coach *Traveller.*

Stroudley's 0–6–0 Terrier Tank (all 24 tons of it).   This engine was
originally the Brighton works pilot.

Coppernob. Bury's 0–4–0 No. 3, designed for the Furness Railway.

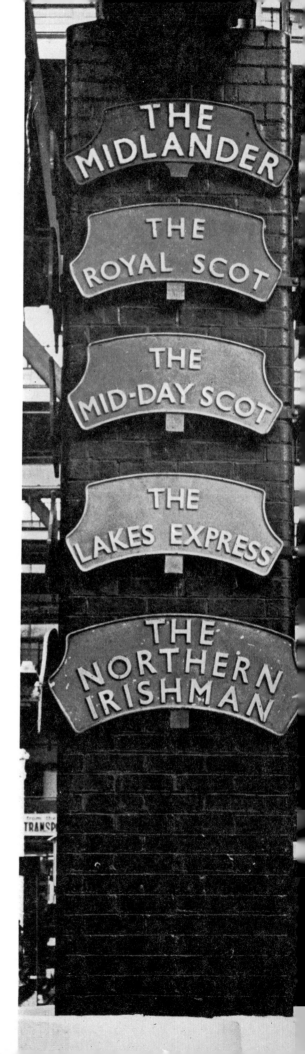

Right: Collection of Nameplates which speak for themselves.

Left: Trevithick's 2–2–2 *Cornwall*, and Johnson's 4–4–0 Compound No. 1000.

Below: "Director" and "Compound". Midland Railway 4–4–0 No. 1000 and Robinson's Large Director 4–4–0 *Butler Henderson*.

York Museum. *Above:* Patrick Stirling's 8-ft bogie single built for the Great Northern Railway.

Right: The Allan single *Columbine*, the first engine built at Crewe.

York Museum. Ivatt's Great Northern Atlantic No. 251.

Above: Re-built Turbo-motive No. 46202 *Princess Anne* at Wavertree, with the up Red Rose Express.

Right: *Princess Anne* is prepared for her journey to London at Edge Hill M.P.D.

Blasting up the hill from Lime Street Station. "Princess" Pacific No.
46208 *Princess Helena Victoria* with the up Shamrock.

Left: "Jubilee" class 4–6–0 No. 45646 *Napier* sets out from Liverpool with a morning train for Hull.

Below: London train makes an energetic start from Lime Street. "Jubilee" class 4–6–0 No. 45581 *Bihar and Orissa.*

Above: Journey's end in Lime Street Station. Stanier Pacific No. 46240 *City of Coventry* arrives with train from Euston.

Below: Journey's beginning at Lime Street Station. Stanier class 5MT 4–6–0 No. 44773 sets out with a train for the West of England.

Two more in the cutting.
Left: "Re-built Scot" No. 46138 *London Irish Rifleman* starts the climb with the up Merseyside Express.

Below: "Royal Scot" engine before re-building almost at the top with up London train. No. 6130 *West Yorkshire Regiment.*

Left: Passing the old Edge Hill No. 2 Box, "Jubilee" class 4–6–0 No. 45587 *Baroda* with a morning train for London.

Below: Winding through Edge Hill Station, Re-built "Patriot" No. 45527 *Southport* heads south with the up Merseyside Express.

Above: Rounding the curve past Edge Hill Sheds. No. 46200 *Princess Royal* with the up Manxman.

Below: A "Duchess" in its original condition, before fitting of double chimney and smoke deflectors. No. 6231 *Duchess of Atholl* at Wavertree Junction.

Left: Liverpool to Newcastle train at Wavertree. Stanier class 5MT No. 45075. The line for London bends off to the left.

Below: Morning train for Birmingham at Picton Road, Wavertree. "Patriot" 4–6–0 No. 45518 *Bradshaw.*

Above: Stanier 5MT 4–6–0 No. 45418 passes Edge Hill Sheds with afternoon train for Shrewsbury and South Wales.

Left: "Princess" Pacific No. 46208 *Princess Helena Victoria* at the coaling plant: Edge Hill Motive Power Depot.

Below: "Patriot" No. 5523 *Bangor* at Edge Hill. Photo taken before re-building.

Left: A1 Pacific No. 60153 *Flamboyant* at platform 15 York Station with a train for Newcastle.

Below: Neck and Neck out of York. D49/2 4–4–0 No. 62772 *The Sinnington* with train from Scarborough to Leeds, and class 5MT 4–6–0 No. 44811 heads a train for Birmingham.

Above: Scene in the engine repair shops at York.

Right: "Britannia" Pacific No. 70035 *Rudyard Kipling* in the engine yard at York.

Below: A1 Pacific No. 60138 *Boswell* (name-plates removed) and a V2 2–6–2 in the Round-house at York.

Top: Trio at York. A2 Pacific No. 60526 *Sugar Palm*: A1 Pacific No. 60121 *Silurian*: and Class D20 4–4–0 No. 62388.

Centre: Class J94 0–6–0 reverses a coal train into the St. Helen's goods yards at York.

Below: The Station Pilot at York. Class J71 0–6–0T No. 68280.

Above: Newcastle to Liverpool train leaves York. A3 Pacific No. 60082 *Neil Gow.*

Right: Scarborough to Leeds train leaves York behind a pair of "Hunt" class 4–4–0s.

Below: A pair of "Jubilee" 4–6–0s head the afternoon empty stock train through York.

Right: A2/3 Pacific No. 60518 *Tehran* changes crews at York on its way north.

Below: Freight train at Poppleton. B16 4–6–0 No. 61471.

Right: Newcastle train sets out from York. A1 Pacific No. 60127 *Wilson Wordsell.*

Above: "Stand-by" engine at York. Class A2/2 Pacific No. 60502 *Earl Marischal*.

Left: Along the level between Darlington and York. Class A2/3 Pacific No. 60513 *Dante* with an up Newcastle express.

Below: Cautiously through York Station. A4 Pacific No. 60014 *Silver Link* with the down Elizabethan.

Top: Ex W.D. 2–8–0 No. 90162 pulls into the York North goods yard with a train from the north.

Centre: Maid of all work! Class V2 2–6–2 No. 60839 belts out of York with a train from East Anglia to Newcastle.

Bottom: A "Director" class 4–4–0 pulls out of York with an evening train for Sheffield. Class D11/1 No. 62663 *Prince Albert.*

Above: Encounter South of Crewe. The up Royal Scot behind a "Duchess" Pacific meets the Birmingham to Glasgow train worked by "Princess" Pacific No. 46212 *Duchess of Kent.*

Right: The down Red Rose approaches Crewe from the south. Re-built "Patriot" No. 45521 *Rhyl.*

Above: Manchester to Euston train pulls out of Manchester London Road behind "Britannia" Pacific No. 70032 *Tennyson.*

Below left: Class C14 4–4–2T No. 67441 leaves London Road with a local train for Guide Bridge.

Below right: Mid-day train for Euston gets away behind "Jubilee" class No. 45578 *United Provinces* and class 4MT 2–6–4T No. 42494.

147

Above: A3 Pacific No. 60103 *Flying Scotsman* storms up the bank at Copley Hill with an express for King's Cross.

Left: A4 Pacific No. 60007 *Sir Nigel Gresley* approaches Ardsley with morning train from Leeds to King's Cross.

Leeds City Station.

Right: Train from Newcastle to Liverpool, after reversing, sets a westerly course. "Patriot" No. 45519 *Lady Godiva* pilots rebuilt "Scot" No. 46124 *London Scottish*.

Left: A3 Pacific No. 60036 *Colombo* at the east end of the Station with North Briton.

Right: Class 5MT 4–6–0 No. 45060 sets out with a stopping train for Manchester. D49 4–4–0 No. 62727 *The Quorn* with a train for Harrogate.

Right: Andrew K. McCosh (who was he?) A4 No. 60003 pulls out of Leeds Central with train for King's Cross.

Above: Class C13 4–4–2T No. 67433 passes Holbeck with a train for Pontefract.

Right: A3 Pacific No. 60086 *Gainsborough* slips on a greasy rail with the down Queen of Scots at Leeds Central.

Above: A4 Pacific No. 60026 *Miles Beevor*, with steam to spare, pulls out of Leeds Central with the up Yorkshire Pullman.

Right: The up White Rose sets out for London. A3 Pacific No. 60046 *Diamond Jubilee* struggles up the bank to Holbeck.

Above: The down Thames–Clyde Express leaves Leeds City. "Rebuilt Scot" No. 46112 *Sherwood Forester.*

Right: The up Thames–Clyde Express at Wortley Junction. "Britannia" Pacific No. 70054 *Dornoch Firth.*

Above: The down Waverley leaves Leeds City. "Jubilee" class 4–6–0 No. 45694 *Bellerophon*.

Right: The up Waverley at Wortley Junction. "Jubilee" class 4–6–0 No. 45619 *Nigeria*.

Above: Class O2 2–8–0 No. 63985 coasts down the hill at Beeston with coal train.

Below: Gresley Pacific No. 4472 *Flying Scotsman* leaves Wakefield Kirkgate with a special for Llandudno, organised by the Gainsborough Model Railway Society.

Above: The Liverpool to Newcastle winds across the tracks at Wortley Junction. A3 Pacific No. 60077 *The White Knight*.

Below: A bit of free advertising on the front of A3 Pacific No. 60056 *Centenary* on the up White Rose.

Top: The Morecambe Residential at Wortley Junction. "Jubilee" 4–6–0 No. 45605 *Cyprus.*

Left: Class 4MT 2–6–4T No. 42141 rounds the curve out of Leeds City with a train from Bristol to Bradford.

Below: Bradford portion of London train passes Beeston on its way to Wakefield where it will join the Leeds portion. 4–6–4T No. 42141.

Above: Framed in the signal gantry at Wortley South, A1 Pacific No. 60117 *Bois Roussel* with the up Queen of Scots Pullman.

Left: Compound 4–4–0 No. 41080 leaves Leeds City with train for Sheffield.

Below: Liverpool to Newcastle train at Whitehall Junction. A3 Pacific No. 60077 *The White Knight*.

Evening at Wortley South. A4 Pacific No. 60008 *Dwight D. Eisenhower* with an express bound for King's Cross.

Morning at Wortley South. A3 Pacific No. 60051 *Blink Bonny* with the up Yorkshire Pullman.

Above: The down Thames–Clyde Express at Wortley Junction. "Rebuilt Scot" No. 46130 *West Yorkshire Regiment*.

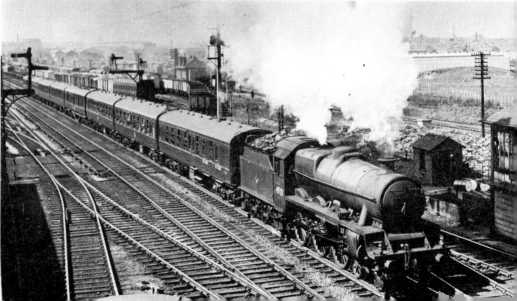

Right: The up Waverley at Durran Hill, Carlisle. "Jubilee" class 4–6–0 No. 45711 *Courageous*.

Left: The up Waverley starts after the Skipton stop. Class 5MT No. 44852.

Below: The down Waverley at Bell Busk. "Britannia" Pacific No. 70053 *Moray Firth.*

Ribblehead Viaduct.

Top: View from footplate of "Britannia" Pacific No. 70054 *Dornoch Firth*.

Centre: A "Jubilee" 4–6–0 nips down the hill with the up Waverley.

Bottom: Northbound freight train crosses the viaduct under the shadow of Whernside.

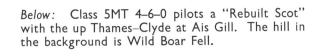

Above: With Ingleborough in the background a "Jubilee" approaches Blea Moor with the down Waverley.

Left: A3 Pacific No. 60081 *Shotover* plunges into Blea Moor tunnel with Leeds to Glasgow train.

Below: Class 5MT 4–6–0 pilots a "Rebuilt Scot" with the up Thames–Clyde at Ais Gill. The hill in the background is Wild Boar Fell.

Nearing the top of the climb to Ais Gill from the north. Class 4F 0–6–0 No. 44512.

Class 9F 2–10–0 No. 92139 takes it easy after the climb to Ais Gill.

Below: "Crab" 2–6–0 No. 42843 in the Mallerstang Valley with empty stock train.

Above: With the Northern Pennines in the background "Re-built Scot" No. 46117 *Welsh Guardsman* near Kirkby Stephen with the up Waverley.

Below: Class 2P 4–4–0 No. 40615 pilots a class 5MT 4–6–0 with the up Waverley north of Kirkby Stephen.

Above: Before re-building, Royal Scot engine No. 46148 *The Manchester Regiment* passes Preston with a parcels train.

Below: Fowler built 2–6–4T No. 42317 on the curve to the north of Preston Station with a train for Blackpool.

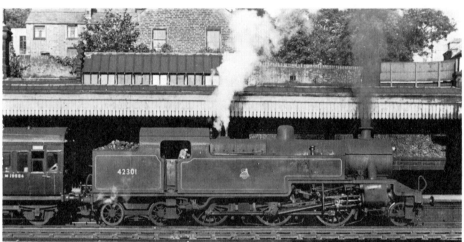

Above: Crossing the Ribble at Preston. Re-built "Patriot" No. 45534. *E. Tootal Broadhurst* with Perth–Euston train.

Right: Fowler built 2–6–4T No. 42301 at Lancaster with a local train.

Below: Class 5MT 4–6–0 No. 45439 dashes up the bank from Lancaster Station with southbound freight.

Above: Barrow to Euston train leaves Lancaster Station. "Jubilee" 4–6–0 No. 45689 *Ajax*.

Below: Glasgow to Manchester train pulls away from Lancaster. B.R. Light Pacific No. 72000 *Clan Buchanan*. Lancaster Castle and Priory in the background.

Oxenholme. *Above:* An unidentified class 5 4–6–0 stops with a Glasgow to Liverpool train.

Below: Pacific No. 46239 *City of Chester* sets off into the hill country with a London to Carlisle train.

Grayrigg.

I. Class 8F 2–8–0 No. 48435 with northbound freight.

II. "Princess" Pacific No. 46211 *Queen Maud* coasts down the hill with Glasgow to Birmingham train.

Below: III. "Britannia" Pacific No. 70050 *Firth of Clyde* with morning train for Perth.

The Lune Valley. *Above:* I. A freight train goes north.

Below left: II. "Jubilee" No. 45561 *Saskatchewan* near Low Gill with a fitted freight.

Below right: III. A "Re-built Scot" takes more water than it needs from the troughs at Dillicar. No. 46121 *Highland Light Infantry.*

Above: **The Lune Valley.** IV. Class 4F 0–6–0 jogs along the valley with a train of iron ore empties.

Left: Banking on Shap. 2–6–4T No. 42404 gives a helping shove to a freight train.

Below: Class 2F 0–6–0 *"Cauliflower"* No. 58409 near Troutbeck between Keswick and Penrith with a coal train: Blencathra in the background.

Above: Approaching Shap Summit. "Princess" Pacific No. 46207 *Princess Arthur of Connaught* with Birmingham to Glasgow train.

Below: The up Coronation at Thrimby. Pacific No. 6223 *Princess Alice*.

Above: Perth to Euston train passes Thrimby Grange box. Class 7P "Jubilee" 4–6–0 No. 45736 *Phoenix*, rebuilt with larger boiler and double chimney.

Right: A "Patriot" and a "Britannia" coasting down the hill towards Penrith with safety valves blowing.

Below: Tail end view of the up Royal Scot at Clifton.

Above: "Jubilee" No. 45593 *Kolhapur* leans to the curve at Penrith Station with empty stock and parcels train.

Below: "Down in the woods something . . . puffed." "Princess" Pacific No. 46208 *Princess Helena Victoria* in the woods at Great Strickland with Glasgow to Birmingham train.

Above: "Britannia" Pacific No. 70050 *Firth of Clyde* in the Strickland woods, heads a train for Manchester from Glasgow.

Below: Up mid-day Scot at Thrimby. Pacific No. 46248 *City of Leeds*.

Top: City of Sheffield, Pacific No. 46249 pulls out of Carlisle Citadel with Glasgow to Birmingham train.

Centre: Afternoon train for Perth at Etterby, north of Carlisle. "Princess" Pacific No. 46203 *Princess Margaret Rose.*

Bottom: Smoke *not* by arrangement! "Patriot" No. 45502 *Royal Naval Division* pilots "Jubilee" 4–6–0 on a train for Manchester from Glasgow.

Above: Sunlight and shadow in Carlisle Citadel. "Jubilee" No. 45630 *Swaziland* moves out with train from Edinburgh to St. Pancras.

Right: With Carlisle Cathedral in the background, "Jubilee" No. 45726 *Vindictive* leaves with a train for Edinburgh.

Below: "Rebuilt" Scot No. 46117 *Welsh Guardsman* arrives at Carlisle with train from Leeds to Glasgow. "Jubilee" No. 45716 *Swiftsure* waits for its train on the middle road.

Above: Up Thames–Clyde Express at Durran Hill, Carlisle. Class 5MT No. 44673 pilots "Jubilee" 4–6–0 No. 45619 *Nigeria*.

Above: Princess Margaret Rose No. 46203 heads north past Kingmoor Sheds with afternoon train for Perth.

Below: Leeds to Glasgow train leaves Carlisle. A3 Pacific No. 60081 *Shotover*.

Above: B1 4-6-0 No. 61145 takes the Waverley route from Carlisle with freight train for Millerhill.

Right: Passing at Upperby. Pacific No. 46221 *Queen Elizabeth* on the up Royal Scot meets "Rebuilt Scot" No. 46136 *The Border Regiment* on a train from Manchester to Glasgow.

Below: Class J39 0-6-0 No. 64932 with a train for Silloth at Canal Junction, Carlisle.

Left: Up Flying Scotsman at Gateshead. A4 Pacific No. 60023 *Golden Eagle.*

Below: An A3 Pacific creeps across the King Edward VIIth Bridge with a northbound fitted freight.

Facing page top: View from the Keep. The down Talisman leaving Newcastle Central for Edinburgh. A4 Pacific No. 60012 *Commonwealth of Australia.*

Facing page bottom: Under the old signal gantry at Newcastle. A3 Pacific No. 60092. *Fairway* leaves with a train from Newcastle to Bristol.

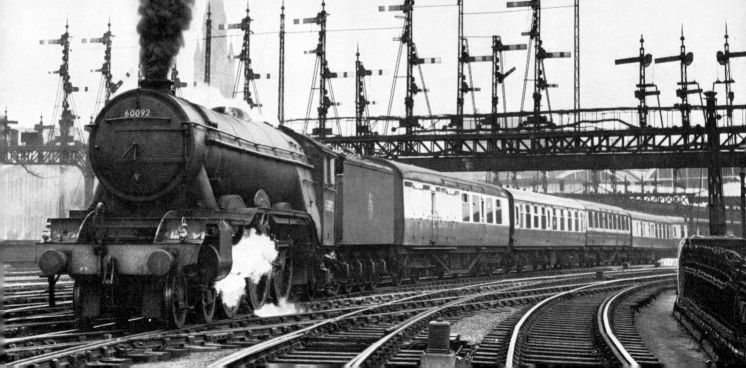

Above: Bound for Bristol from Newcastle. A3 Pacific No. 60080 *Dick Turpin* on the approach to the King Edward Bridge.

Below: Coming off the King Edward Bridge. A4 Pacific No. 60031 *Golden Plover* rounds the bend at Gateshead with the up Elizabethan.

Above: 46201 *Princess Elizabeth* at Harthope on Beattock with the down Royal Scot.

Left: At the bottom of the Bank. Beattock station with a banker returning from the summit.

Above: "Jubilee" No. 45698 *Mars* sets out from Beattock Station with a train from Manchester to Glasgow.

Left: "Britannia" Pacific No. 70050 *Firth of Clyde* near Greskine with a train for Perth.

Up the wooded slopes of Beattock.   Class 5MT 4–6–0 with a coal train.

Above: Glasgow to Birmingham train near Elvanfoot, on the northward approach to Beattock Summit. "Princess" Pacific No. 46212 *Duchess of Kent.*

Below: The down Scot at Harthope. Pacific No. 46250 *City of Lichfield.*

A "Black Stanier" No. 44878 climbs steadily to Beattock Summit, with
a train for Perth.

Above: Passing Greskine signal box with the down Royal Scot. Pacific No. 46240 *City of Coventry.*

Below: In the Clyde valley. Up mid-day Scot passes Abington Station. Pacific No. 46252 *City of Leicester.*

Right: The last of the "Royal Scots" to be re-built. No. 46137 *The Prince of Wales Volunteers (South Lancs)* chugs up Beattock with a Scottish express.

Passing Beattock Summit Box with the up Mid-day Scot. "Princess" Pacific No. 46210 *Lady Patricia*.

Pickersgill (ex-Caledonian) class 3P 4–4–0 No. 54490 coasts down from Beattock Summit with northbound freight.

The up Royal Scot at Beattock Summit. "Duchess"
Pacific No. 46230 *Duchess of Buccleuch*.

Above: Glasgow Central to Carlisle train approaches Carstairs. "Jubilee" 4–6–0 No. 45645 *Collingwood*.

Left: In sight of the top. No. 46212 *Duchess of Kent* approaches Beattock Summit with the up mid-day Scot.

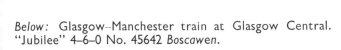

Above: B.R. Standard class 5MT 4–6–0 No. 73061 at Law Junction with a stopping train to Carstairs.

Right: Train for Carlisle leaves Glasgow Central. "Jubilee" 4–6–0 No. 45563 *Australia*.

Below: Glasgow–Manchester train at Glasgow Central. "Jubilee" 4–6–0 No. 45642 *Boscawen*.

Above: BI 4–6–0 No. 61191 at Galashiels with a freight train.

Left: Carlisle to Edinburgh Waverley train at Shankend. A2 Pacific No. 60527 *Sun Chariot.*

Right: Labouring up the Cockburnspath Bank. Class V2 2–6–2 No. 60806 at Penmanshiel with freight train.

Centre: Edinburgh Waverley to Hawick train at Falahill Summit. B1 4–6–0 No. 61385.

Bottom: Freight train approaches Hawick. K3 class 2–6–0 No. 61916.

Left: K3 class 2–6–0 No. 61981 at Hawick Station with freight train.

Centre: In sight of the sea. A4 Pacific No. 60024 *Kingfisher* near Burnmouth with the down Elizabethan.

Bottom: Glasgow to King's Cross train at Portobello East. A4 Pacific No. 60022 *Mallard*.

Above: In Princes Street Station, Edinburgh, "Duchess" Pacific No. 46231 *Duchess of Atholl* with stopping train to Glasgow.

Below: In Waverley Station, Edinburgh. Class D11 4–4–0 No. 62678 *Luckie Mucklebackit* on a train for Dundee.

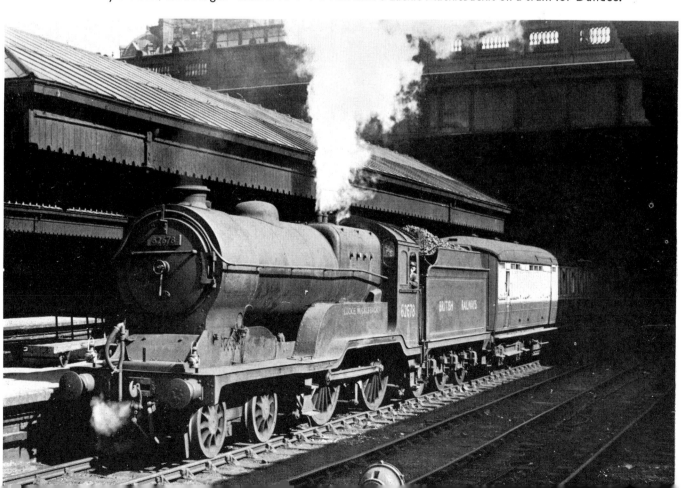

Above: The down Elizabethan at Grantshouse. A4 Pacific No. 60034 *Lord Faringdon.*

Left: Laying the dust at Edinburgh Waverley. A3 Pacific No. 60041 *Salmon Trout.*

Below: In the Princes Street Gardens, Edinburgh. The North Briton on the last stage of its journey to Glasgow. A3 Pacific No. 60090 *Grand Parade.*

Above: West end of Waverley Station. Train for Aberdeen leaves behind A3 Pacific.

Right: A4 Pacific No. 60010 *Dominion of Canada* sets out from Waverley with Glasgow to King's Cross train.

Below: Class J38 0–6–0 No. 65920 emerges from Calton Tunnel with freight train.

Above: Victorian Masterpiece. The Forth Railway Bridge from South Queensferry.

Left: Up aloft. An unusual view of A1 Pacific No. 60160 *Auld Reekie* with a fish train on the Forth Bridge.

Summer's evening at Edinburgh Waverley.   Class J83 0–6–0T
No. 68481 takes water at the West end of the Station.

Above: Evening train from Edinburgh to Glasgow passing Haymarket Sheds. A3 Pacific No. 60087 *Blenheim.*

Below: Glasgow to King's Cross train in Edinburgh Waverley. A4 Pacific No. 60009 *Union of South Africa.*

Above: Morning at Princes Street Station, Edinburgh. 2–4–6T No. 42204 assists a "Jubilee" 4–6–0 with a train for Liverpool and Manchester.

Right: Departure from St. Enoch, Glasgow. Class 2P 4–4–0 No. 40579 with a train for Ardrossan.

Below: "Rebuilt Scot" No. 46117 *Welsh Guardsman* starts the up Thames–Clyde Express out of Kilmarnock.

Dumfries.

I *Top left:* "Britannia" Pacific No. 70044 *Earl Haig* starts the up Thames–Clyde Express out of Dumfries.

II *Top right:* B.R. standard class 5MT and a "Crab" 2–6–0 pull out of the Dumfries goods yards with the northbound freight.

III *Above right:* View of Dumfries Shed. Class 5 4–6–0 No. 44895 and class 2F 0–6–0 Drummond Caledonian goods Engine No. 57267.

IV *Right:* Drummond 0–6–0 goods engine approaches Dumfries from the Stranraer line.

Below: Coal train at New Cumnock. "Crab" 2–6–0 No. 42729.

Above: Stopping train to Glasgow St. Enoch leaves Dumfries. "Jubilee" Class 4–6–0 No. 45691 *Orion.*

Right: Up Thames–Clyde Express approaches Dumfries. "Rebuilt Scot" No. 46109 *Royal Engineer.*

Below: Class VI 2–6–2T No. 67610 enters Dalmeny Station with a train from Dundee. Forth Bridge in the background.

In the "West Highlands" country.

I *Above:* Black Stanier 4–6–0 No. 45499 leaves Fort William with morning train for Glasgow.

II *Left:* Class K2/2, 2–6–0 No. 61789 *Loch Laidon* pulls out of Fort William yards with cattle train.

In the "West Highlands" country.

III *Right:* Beside the shores of Loch Linnhe K2 2–6–0 No. 61771 leaves Fort William for Mallaig.

IV *Below:* On the Mallaig Extension. K2 2–6–0s No. 61787 *Loch Quoich* and No. 61771 with afternoon train for Glasgow.

V *Right:* The Road to the Isles: morning train for Mallaig sets out from Fort William. K1/1 2–6–0 No. 61997.

In the "West Highlands" country.

VI *Above:* K2 2–6–0 No. 61788 *Loch Rannoch* eases out of Fort William yards with a train of very mixed traffic.

VII *Left:* In the Monessie Gorge. K4 2–6–0 No. 61996 *Lord of the Isles* puffs up the hill from Spean Bridge.

VIII *Below:* Same day, same train! *Lord of the Isles* glides through the station at Tulloch.

The end of the Skye Line.

I *Above:* McIntosh 0–4–4T No. 55216 shunting at Kyle of Lochalsh. The mountains of Skye in background.

II *Right:* Class 5MT No. 45179 leaves the "Kyle" for Inverness with morning train.

III *Below left:* The "Kyle" shunter marshalling a cattle train.

IV *Below right:* Class 5MT 4–6–0 sets out on, perhaps, the most beautiful scenic route in the British Isles from Kyle of Lochalsh to Inverness.

Top: Morning Scene at the "Kyle". Class 5MT brews up on the Inverness train, and one of MacBrayne's steamers waits at the quay before leaving for the Western Isles.

Centre: Rounding the shore of Loch Carron, near Plockton, class 5MT 4–6–0 No. 44783 with train for Inverness.

Bottom: Freight train from Inverness entering Achnasheen. Class 5MT 4–6–0 No. 45098.